J. TED O

$30 MILLION AND BROKE

IF YOU HAVE IT, DON'T LOSE IT

RIVER GROVE
BOOKS

This publication is designed to provide accurate and authoritative information in regard to the subject matter covered. It is sold with the understanding that the publisher and author are not engaged in rendering legal, accounting, or other professional services. Nothing herein shall create an attorney-client relationship, and nothing herein shall constitute legal advice or a solicitation to offer legal advice. If legal advice or other expert assistance is required, the services of a competent professional should be sought.

The testimonial provided by Dan Kennedy on the back cover was provided by a current client of Oxbow Advisors. The client was not compensated, nor are there material conflicts of interest that would affect the given statement. The statement may not be representative of the experience of other current clients and does not provide a guarantee of future performance success or similar services.

Published by River Grove Books
Austin, TX
www.rivergrovebooks.com

Copyright © 2024 Oxbow Advisors

All rights reserved.

Thank you for purchasing an authorized edition of this book and for complying with copyright law. No part of this book may be reproduced, stored in a retrieval system, or transmitted by any means, electronic, mechanical, photocopying, recording, or otherwise, without written permission from the copyright holder.

Distributed by River Grove Books

Design and composition by Greenleaf Book Group
Cover design by Greenleaf Book Group
Cover images used under license from ©Shutterstock.com/Nomad_Soul

Publisher's Cataloging-in-Publication data is available.

Print ISBN: 978-1-63299-848-4

eBook ISBN: 978-1-63299-849-1

First Edition

To Grayson, Worth, Cooper, and Ellie

And to my old friend Frank Knapp Jr., who taught me the benefit of writing

ABOUT OXBOW ADVISORS

At Oxbow Advisors, we've spent 40 years working with people who've gained significant first-generation wealth and are trying to maximize it across future generations. Many of these individuals have experienced liquidity events, and they depend on our knowledge and experience to help them navigate the steps that will lead to lasting, cross-generational wealth.

What we do is simple, but hard to find in today's investment world:

We protect the wealth you worked hard to create.

If you would like more information, call 512-386-1088 or visit www.OxbowAdvisors.com

CONTENTS

PREFACE vii

   CHAPTER 1: Why Does It Happen? 1

   CHAPTER 2: How Did They Get the Money? 5

   CHAPTER 3: Athletes, Movie Stars, and
   Lottery Winners—All Broke 11

   CHAPTER 4: Extreme Loss and the Everyday Millionaire 17

   CHAPTER 5: Lack of Appreciation for Wealth 23

   CHAPTER 6: Beware the Ego 29

   CHAPTER 7: The Big Deal 33

   CHAPTER 8: The Trouble with Family Money 37

CHAPTER 9: The Trouble with the Family Business 45

CHAPTER 10: Feeding the Animals 49

CHAPTER 11: Concentration in One Stock 53

CHAPTER 12: Listening to Wall Street Hype 57

CHAPTER 13: The Base Capital/Investment Capital Divide 65

CHAPTER 14: The Biggest Need: Understanding Risk 71

CHAPTER 15: Lifestyle Changes 79

CHAPTER 16: Hard to Make, Harder to Keep 85

CHAPTER 17: Money, Purpose, Friends—and Mortality 95

CHAPTER 18: If You Have It, Don't Lose It 99

CONCLUSION 103

KEY CHARACTERISTICS OF OXBOW ADVISORS 105

ABOUT THE AUTHOR 107

PREFACE

Going from rags to riches is the American dream, and it happens, nearly every day, to someone. I should know—even though it's been quite a long time since the day I was the one. I made the transition the hard way, over inches and years, by way of humbling jobs, false starts, and at least my fair share of failures. It took a long while, but from the time I was six years old, I knew that if I wanted anything—even basics like shoes on my feet, a bed that was mine, or a trip to a barber or a dentist—I'd have to get it on my own.

Fast forward four decades, and I find myself in the privileged position of meeting, observing, and advising thousands of others who've walked the rags-to-riches road. They come through the door at Oxbow Advisors, the investment firm I founded, flush with enough money to support them and their families in perpetuity. Many are business owners; some are heirs; others are athletes and artists with unique talents and big contracts. A few are lottery winners or settlement recipients. What they all have in common are bright futures and deep pockets.

In my years in business, I've watched markets move, fads come and go, and entire industries rise and fall. But for all that has changed, one thing never does: A significant percentage of the people who've gained set-for-life wealth—$30 million, $50 million, $100 million, $200 million, or more—will soon lose it all. They'll live out the reverse of the American dream—going from riches to rags. I can tell you in all honesty that when you're up close and personal, watching those stories play out, it knots your stomach. The unnecessary waste and misery of lost fortunes is ugly business, and in every one of those stories, someone ends up with their pockets turned out, wondering how they could have been so foolish and careless.

Times change, but this roller coaster of loss does not. It's as much a fact of life in the investment world as death and taxes.

Here's one other thing that stays the same: No investor ever sets out claiming, "If I had 30 million dollars, I'd go broke." Of course not. We all think that if and when it's our turn to have that kind of money, we won't blow it. It'd be impossible. It *should* be impossible. And yet there are people from every walk of life who've ended up seeing their millions go up in smoke. Once in a while I meet a rare member of this club who's made it all back and then

PREFACE

some, but most of the stories end badly—with drastic changes in life and lifestyle, personal devastation, and deep humiliation.

It's not enough to tell investors to stay vigilant. After decades of watching this pattern repeat over and over again, I want to get specific about why it happens and how to keep it from happening to you.

This book is full of stories of real people who didn't use their heads when it came to money. You'll meet individuals, couples, and multi-generational families who went from riches to rags. All of us know someone who is, at this very moment, going through money like water down a drain. We have a pretty good idea what the end of their story will look like. If this book could help even one of those people get it together before they crash and burn, it'll have been worth the effort.

Whether you're seeking to safeguard your own fortune or looking out for someone close to you, I hope you can use the information here to your benefit.

I'd like to thank Kim Mathis-Doumis for her unending efforts in helping me on this project, my wonderful staff at Oxbow for their dedication to safeguarding fortunes, my editor Jana Murphy, and, most of all, the Oxbow clients from whom I am always learning.

—Ted Oakley

Chapter 1

WHY DOES IT HAPPEN?

All of us have heard stories of people who accumulated or inherited large sums of money, only to end up with little or nothing. Once in a while this scenario happens to someone who came into their fortune so fast it feels a little like fate: easy come, easy go. But too often the whole story reads a bit like a long, excruciating trek to a mountaintop. For years or decades, a person works and sacrifices, building a business and inching higher. When they sell that business for a fortune, they've reached the pinnacle. The ones who are careful and wise with their wealth can stay up there a long time and enjoy the experience. But the ones who can't temper their spending, manage their risk, or control their egos don't find satisfaction. They start sliding backward almost as soon as they arrive.

For many years I've been intrigued and saddened by this phenomenon. The tales are endless: entrepreneurs, kids of baby boomers, online millionaires, professional athletes, and many others—all of whom lost fortunes. Sometimes the only thing they have in common is the demoralizing trip from having everything to owning next to nothing. Anyone who's looking at this situation from the outside wants to know the *why* and *how*. We want to feel confident it couldn't happen to us. We think maybe they got mixed up with a shady business partner. Maybe they self-sabotaged because they felt unworthy. Maybe they had a mile-wide reckless streak and nobody around to temper it. Maybe they were addicted to spending. Maybe some habit or mindset from childhood guided their decisions instead of good sense. Maybe they chose a spectacularly bad advisor. Maybe, after working their entire lives to build financial security, they'd rather blow it all than say *no* to their children.

Or maybe they just quit thinking straight.

Even after 40 years of counseling investors, I still haven't found one common denominator that tells the whole story. And I continue to be saddened at what goes through the minds of these people who've failed at wealth, of all things. They're wracked by guilt, shame, sorrow, remorse, and worry for their families.

There are no easy discussions on this subject, and yet we need to talk about it. Becoming educated about the dangers and pitfalls of managing the wealth is the best way to arm against them. With that in mind, my hope in writing *$30 Million and Broke* is threefold:

- To explore the question of why it happens and offer some answers.

- To share a seasoned advisor's perspective on the issue of squandered wealth.

- To help readers—especially those who've recently sold a business and come into newly liquid wealth—avoid going down this long, miserable road.

The entry point to preventing wealth loss is learning that it could happen to anyone, but it's *most likely* to happen to an investment novice who comes at the practice with the attitude of a know-it-all. Just like any other field, investment is a learned skill, one with elements of both science and art and one in which experience is the ultimate teacher.

It's just common sense to come at this process with caution, but too many wealthy investors don't realize it until they experience a blistering loss—and some don't even learn then. It seems that many of them are intent on being "right," even if it means losing their entire nest egg.

In 1587, Dr. John Bridge of England wrote: "A fool and his money [are] soon parted." More than 400 years later, the good doctor is still right.

As you go through this book, you'll see all types of investors. Many of them are the kinds of people we've seen over the years at Oxbow Advisors. I'm reminded of the investor who sold a business, immediately opened a vineyard in California, and then watched the whole thing implode. By the time the storm was over, he was left with no fortune, no business, and no home.

Or the businessman in the Southeast who decided to let his "smart" children run his assets. When he finally checked in to see how that was working out, he discovered they'd lost a bundle of money, mostly because they didn't have the backbone to turn down the latest "hot deal."

In addition to sharing some of my own experiences, I've interviewed great entrepreneurs, executives, CPAs, estate lawyers, and some just plain smart people. Their insights help me shed light on this curious, fascinating, and poignant subject.

I've always considered each loss of fortune a cautionary tale, and I recommend the investors who seek my advice do the same. Each of us only goes around once in life. Having financial resources doesn't guarantee happiness, but it's far easier to navigate the good times and the bad with your balance sheet intact.

Chapter 2

HOW DID THEY GET THE MONEY?

How people end up with wealth has some implications for what they do with it. As you can imagine, the individual with $30 million built by decades of sweat equity, personal risk, and dedication tends to see the world from a different vantage point than one who makes a meteoric rise over a year or two. And both of them bring different baggage to having money than their peers who were born to wealth and inherited their millions. Each group has its to-hell-with-convention members, and each has those who invest by the book (though which book can have a profound impact on their outcome). That said, over the years the advisors at Oxbow and I have seen some patterns in the people who make it into the exclusive club. Consider each group:

THE BUSINESS BUILDERS

Since 1983, I've worked with thousands of multi-millionaires from this group, advising business owners in almost every industry and state. Most of them share a basic trajectory, even though the details vary wildly. They start with an idea, maybe some seed money, and their own two hands. They build a business from nothing, creating both jobs and equity. Many of them have known lean times when they weren't sure if they could make payroll or pay their vendors, but they gutted it out. When they decide to sell, they're blessed with one-time infusions of liquid assets—often in the millions, tens of millions, or more. In many cases, those assets arrive at the same time these individuals find themselves with their calendars wide open and more free time than they've had in decades.

These former business owners are a pleasure to know and work with because they are, by and large, a very astute lot. But even this group is not without some players who blow it all.

THE SHOOTING STARS

This group is also comprised of business builders—and they've created substantial numbers of jobs and significant equity. The difference is that for these individuals it happened in a hurry. Many are dot-com millionaires and tech innovators who came up with game-changing ideas, put them in motion, and then sold off the companies at their first opportunity. From 2015 to 2023 we met a large number of these individuals at Oxbow—many of them under 40. This group has great energy, a can-do spirit, and a track record of success. What they often lack is an appreciation of the fact that lightning rarely strikes twice. Early, huge success can make it easy to think a lost fortune can easily be replaced, but that's rarely the case.

THE CORPORATE CHAMPS

In an age when the idea of company loyalty is sometimes spoken about as a thing of the past, there is still a contingent of multi-millionaires who've made their fortunes through a job. Some are c-suite executives with huge bonuses and generous profit-sharing structures. Some are employees who've accumulated and wisely invested exceptional company stock options. Some are investor-employees who see their corporations through to public offering or takeovers. This is a group who can sometimes be loyal to a fault, tying themselves to corporate strings that put their wealth at risk.

THE INHERITORS

This group typically acquires wealth through cash, businesses, stocks, land, or rights passed down from an older generation (and sometimes through multiple generations). This group is commonly perceived as being unwise and careless with money, but wealth alone does not doom an heir to a troubled life. I frequently meet second-generation investors who were raised to be self-supporting, financially responsible, and altruistic. Sadly, there's another segment of this same group who are just as bad as their reputation—careless and thoughtless about the privilege of wealth or the consequences of their choices. Training by the older generation has a great deal to do with the younger generation's thought processes. In my experience, this is the group at highest risk for losing their wealth, no matter how much it is. The level of risk is extreme regardless of what form the inheritance takes. Suffice it to say that many parents cannot distinguish between a good child and a good businessperson, and that failure costs them dearly.

THE LANDOWNERS

This subset of the inheritors are holders of what is often considered the most sacred asset of wealthy families: land. This tradition dates back centuries. In many cases, as wealth passes from generation to generation, land is the last asset standing and the only remaining source of cash. It happens most when the older generations have been unsuccessful in their business ventures. When the children and grandchildren inherit, they split the property, sell it—and soon all is gone. I've seen this pattern come to pass countless times—children inherit, cash flow drops, and the legacy land starts to look like just plain money. If generations past knew the fate of their beloved land, many would roll over in their graves. The truth is, businesses, land, and estates have always been passed down, but in many cases, the succession process is not thought out sufficiently.

I'm reminded of a couple in their late 20s who came to my office out of the blue almost 25 years ago with a large inheritance of both cash and land. After they left my office, with my advice apparently going in one ear and out the other, I learned that within 14 months they had frittered away every penny and every acre. The assets could have lasted them a lifetime, and yet in just over a year they were right back where they'd started.

The fact is, any type of asset, inherited or earned, can be derailed.

Chapter 3

ATHLETES, MOVIE STARS, AND LOTTERY WINNERS—ALL BROKE

In 2006, I sat in a Pasadena VIP booth and watched the University of Texas beat Southern Cal in the Rose Bowl. The star quarterback, the player who almost singlehandedly won it for UT, was Vince Young. He was chosen high in the subsequent draft and went on to play for the Tennessee Titans for $34 million, including $30 million in endorsement deals. It was a lot of money for the young star from Texas.

Fast-forward just six years to 2012, and Young had reportedly spent it all. In fact, he was deep in debt. In July of 2013, a judge ordered Young to auction off most of his personal possessions to pay up, and Houston police officers duly showed up at his home to inventory his effects. The next time Young made the news was in 2019, when a storage unit full of his football memorabilia was auctioned off after nonpayment of the rent. Helmets, game balls, and even his MVP trophy from that Rose Bowl game went to the highest bidder.

Young accused his former agent and financial planner of fraudulent advising; the planner claimed Young's lavish spending was his downfall; and nobody, except perhaps the woman who bid for the unknown contents of the storage unit, came out ahead.

In fact, more than $30 million was gone.

The whole unfortunate situation—one that surely brought a lot of heartbreak to a talented young man and his family—is all too common. My son, who spent nine years working in National Football League operations, watched it play out again and again in the sport. Owners of professional teams sometimes tell me tales of all the ways players get separated from their assets—among them questionable advisors, hangers-on with "can't miss" investment opportunities, entourages fueling big spending, and even family members lining up on paydays to receive their money.

These athletes are in good company—the same problems plague suddenly successful entertainers, lottery winners, and others who come unprepared to wealth. Many are too inexperienced, too trusting, and too careless with the funds that are coming in so fast it seems like they'll never run out. Consider just a few examples on a list that's almost endless.

- Baseball pitcher Curt Schilling (Philadelphia Phillies, Arizona Diamondbacks, and Boston Red Sox) lost all $50 million he had earned in baseball before filing for bankruptcy.

- Football quarterback Michael Vick (Atlanta Falcons and Philadelphia Eagles) filed for bankruptcy in 2008 after having signed a 10-year, $130 million contract in 2004.

- Heavyweight boxer Mike Tyson declared bankruptcy in 2003—despite earning more than $400 million during his career.

- Television and movie star Johnny Depp testified during a 2022 court hearing that he'd lost $650 million in earnings. Worse yet, after it was gone, he was on the hook with the IRS for $100 million.

- Entertainer Michael Jackson signed a $1 billion recording contract in 1991, but filed for bankruptcy in 2007. Two years later, at the time of his death, he was reportedly $400 million in debt.

- A number of the *Real Housewives*—famed for their wealth and extravagant lifestyles—have made running out of money an unlikely shared hobby. Teresa Giudice, Sonja Morgan, and Kim Zolciak have all gone through alarming, public financial meltdowns.

- William "Bud" Post, who won $16.2 million in Pennsylvania's lottery, lost everything after six wives and runaway spending. He died in 2006. At the time he was receiving a $450 monthly disability check.

There are a number of running themes in these misfortunes. The first and most obvious is lavish spending. The second is foregoing any sincere and informed financial advice. The third is stories of people showing up to "help" these individuals—and then helping themselves to whatever spoils they can find. And the fourth is that each of these riches-to-rags stories is about someone with tenuous future income: the athlete who could get hurt or cut from the team tomorrow; the musician who could go out of style in a heartbeat; and the movie or television star who might never win another role.

You have to wonder—did anybody try to show this group how to hold on to net worth and improve their lots for a lifetime, instead of just a few years?

From the vantage point of an investment advisor, these people are a nightmare. Their combined lack of self-discipline and appreciation of wealth never ends. Worse, many of them seem to carry so much guilt about their huge influx of money that they spend outrageous amounts on family members and friends—way beyond appropriate generosity. They seldom budget and won't dream of cutting back until it's all gone.

There are people from all walks of life and levels of wealth who try to buy self-worth, but it takes on a whole new level of humiliation when it plays out on a world stage. Some, I hope, ultimately realized that self-worth isn't measured in dollars and cents, but in character, integrity, and responsibility.

In truth, pro sports could do more than it now does to help young athletes. Why not defer some of the funds until age 50—a mandatory "hold back" for retirement? How about providing young athletes with courses in money management and requiring (or at least encouraging) them to participate? Why not create an atmosphere of business for these newly minted money warriors?

The entertainment industry could do more to help those who make it figure out how to preserve their wealth, as well. Managers, agents, and attorneys should feel some moral pull to help their stars plan for future rainy days. Fame tends to be fleeting, and short careers on stages and sets are far more the norm than long ones.

For these multi-millionaires, as well as the lottery winners and settlement recipients who come into quick, large sums of money, the essential goal of protecting a portion of that net worth for the long run just never crosses their minds. At Oxbow, we've had countless meetings with newly minted members of the $30-million-and-up club, but our advice often goes unheeded. They just can't fathom losing.

If I could offer these high-flying stars just one piece of advice, it would be this: Save a significant portion of your wealth! You don't need to have a tremendous return if you just protect your savings. Do it to maintain the security and freedom money gives you—for a lifetime instead of for just a short while.

Chapter 4

EXTREME LOSS AND THE EVERYDAY MILLIONAIRE

For every ball player, pop star, lottery winner, or actor who makes and loses a fortune, there are hundreds of regular people who lose one, too. Extreme loss, which I define as 75 percent or more of net worth, can happen to anyone, from any background, at any age. Those losses come in many forms, but a lot of them can be traced right back to each person's favorite deadly sin. I can count on one hand the times I've seen someone lose $30 million or more who hasn't let envy, gluttony, greed, lust, pride, sloth, or wrath assist in their downfall. I don't say that dispassionately. We're all human; we all make mistakes—but some mistakes play out on an epic level.

All you have to do is hold on, but time and again, wealth slips away. Consider just a few common scenarios:

LAND INVESTMENTS

Somewhere in the back of many minds is the idea that land is always a great investment—a foolproof money-maker. Jimmy was a friend of mine in the Southeast who inherited a considerable amount of money. When he decided to develop land, he broke the cardinal rule of investing and went all in. He did it with the recklessness of someone in a high-stakes poker game—as if he wasn't risking enough money to support his family for generations. When the bust of 2008 came along, he was left high and dry, with very little liquidity. His "sure thing" turned out to be his financial downfall. This didn't have to be. In his pursuit of getting even richer, Jimmy lost track of the fact that he already *had* a sure thing. He failed to remember the age-old quote that "cash is king." Without liquidity he was at the mercy of lenders who ate up what was left of his fortune.

Over decades in the investment world, I've seen stories involving ranches, farms, and other property holdings come up again and again. These investments move slowly, and staying power is paramount. Forced liquidation of land is almost always a losing proposition.

BUSINESS INVESTMENTS

Over half a million U.S. businesses go belly-up every year. An estimated 90 percent of startups fail—most within the first five years. Almost every one of these broke businesses started as a decent idea, or even a great one. And yet, for whatever reason—bad timing, tough competition, poor management, labor issues, or one of a thousand others—they didn't work out. It's an all-too-common trend among new multi-millionaires to look around and feel absolutely certain that their business acumen is infallible—that whatever they choose to invest in will take off and prosper.

It rarely works out that way. Knowing one business, or even one industry, simply does not qualify you to know all types. Tread carefully if you decide to go chasing a new fortune—doing so can easily cost you the one you already have.

CHILDREN WHO DEVOUR ASSETS

Evelyn was a client of ours in the Midwest who had a substantial amount of money left to her upon her husband's death. She had one son who was not only spoiled but also of such low self-esteem that he was always looking to prove himself with another "big deal." In a matter of just a few years, he spent all of his mother's money in this fruitless pursuit. When the cash ran out, he even dipped into her lifetime trust.

What's worse is that she allowed it. She couldn't say *no*. This scenario transpires over and over again. The parent succumbs to the child's wishes and ends up with next to nothing. These are the sins of the children visited on their elders rather than the other way around. Eventually, of course, these once-wealthy parents die—and too often it's in a hopeless state with virtually no financial resources left.

SUBSTANCE ABUSE TURMOIL

One of the saddest patterns of extreme loss I've seen comes in the form of drug and alcohol addiction. From time to time we see a pattern where someone with considerable wealth starts using illegal drugs recreationally (or legal ones too liberally) and then gets hooked. After that, it's generally a downward spiral.

Bo was a businessman in the Northeast who sold his company and walked away with many millions. We managed his money for a long while, trying to keep his finances steady while he went down this dangerous and destructive road. Eventually, though, it cost him everything—his new business, his wife, his children, and his fortune.

It also led to a number of years in federal prison. This is an insidious kind of loss that sneaks up on the person it's happening to—even when the people closest to them can clearly see things are falling apart.

EXCESSIVE SPENDING

Ever wonder why most lottery winners seldom have much money a few years after their win—or why many people who win big lawsuit judgments soon end up right back where they started? It's the spending, spending, and more spending that gets most of them. In their quest to find happiness, they spend everything they have, thinking material things will bring them happiness.

The problem with that logic is that happiness is an internal thing, not one you can achieve with consumerism. These individuals never quit spending until "suddenly" it's all gone. Many people who are inexperienced with money can't seem to recognize that even a huge windfall has limits. The math is not complicated: If you inherit $10 million, buy a couple big houses, and then spend $800,000 a year, it won't last long. This happens all the time—even to people who are sitting on enough money to last them until the end of their days.

MARRIAGES AND HEARTBREAKS

Four marriages into his tumultuous love life, a doctor told me he didn't have enough assets to retire. His lifetime income had been substantial, and he'd always enjoyed a luxurious lifestyle. Unfortunately, in his attempts to impress or love (or both) his four wives in turn, he had done precious little to endear himself to them. What he had accomplished was wasting a tremendous amount of his hard-earned wealth. Net worth can take a big hit from multiple marriages.

It's amazing how often money gets people feeling the need to walk down the aisle—and equally amazing how often it leaves them angry, bitter, and regretful when those unions fall apart.

CONFUSING GREED WITH LOGIC

Many, if not most, people who lose massive fortunes have plenty of help doing it. We'll discuss this in detail in later chapters, but there's no way I can sum up the biggest causes of wealth loss without mentioning that if multi-millionaires weren't so quick to believe any investor, advisor, or con artist who comes along and tells them they can have much, *much* more, far fewer of them would go broke.

This list could go on and on. Use your imagination and you'll come up with a few more true-to-life disasters. Regardless of the magnitude of the meltdown—whether it is $20 million, $200 million, or $2 billion lost—the person doing the losing ends up wallowing in the same feelings of incompetence, depression, and shame.

When it comes to extreme loss, know this: Wealth has a way of leaving weak hands and finding strong ones. It's been happening since the beginning of time.

Chapter 5

LACK OF APPRECIATION FOR WEALTH

Accumulating a large sum of wealth in one's lifetime is an extremely rare feat. Consider these facts:

- According to the U.S. Census Bureau, only 3 percent of those who retire in the United States are free of the need for government assistance.

- In 2019, the average American retiree had less than $400,000 in retirement savings, including 401K and IRA accounts. When you look at the median, that number is even less, with those between 62 and 74 holding around $162,000, and those 75 and older at $83,000. These numbers, compiled from Federal Reserve data, put a fine point on just how rare and exceptional it is to achieve significant wealth. In fact, when you raise the floor of these calculations to a $5 million nest egg, the percentage who hit the mark dwindles to *.01 percent*—just a tiny fraction of the population.

With those stats in mind, there's no denying it's important to stop and appreciate wealth. It doesn't happen to everyone. It doesn't come easily. It shouldn't be squandered. And yet, I believe that most of those who lay waste to their fortunes have a complete lack of appreciation for what it takes to put together large sums of cash.

Some among this crowd are those who inherit, especially those who inherit while they're young. I'll discuss this group in some detail in Chapters 8 and 9, but they can't be ignored here. It's tough to appreciate what you didn't earn—or even to perceive it as a scarce resource. I find that these investors tend to come in two distinct groups: the spenders and the penny-pinchers. The spenders just keep spending money and assume it will last forever. They seem to have no understanding as to where the wealth came from. Over and over they pull money out of their accounts and spend. In time they have little left, and major lifestyle changes must occur.

LACK OF APPRECIATION FOR WEALTH

I recall a case of a young woman who inherited a considerable amount of money from both parents. I quickly realized that she was going to outspend her portfolio in a hurry, but in conversations with her, I learned she had no concept of what life was going to be like without money. She simply couldn't fathom it. To her, wealth was as much of a given as sunlight—something provided by the world. How she could remain ignorant of the way the other 99.9 percent of people live is a mystery, but I can tell you she ended up virtually destitute. She had to start a whole new life before she reached middle age—one in which money no longer appeared whenever she wanted it.

On the other hand, you have inheritors who spend very little and pinch every penny. Sadly, since they have almost no understanding of investing, they continually chase the latest fund manager or the trendiest stock. Much of their information is theoretical in nature and simply not practical. They often lose out because they don't have the ability to sort financial wheat from chaff and make good decisions. They refuse to embrace the need to learn about the building blocks of wealth.

In truth, the greatest mystery to me and to my fellow advisors at Oxbow isn't about those who inherit large sums. It's the lack of appreciation from some individuals who've built their fortunes brick by brick. The progression from starting a business to breaking even; from turning a profit to maintaining that profit against the heavy burdens of taxes; from making a margin to amassing significant liquid wealth—it's typically a long, rough road. In fact, few people ever navigate it successfully.

And yet, outside of the framework of their businesses and new to the investment world, some of these same financial pioneers and notable successes suddenly become careless instead of calculated. They develop amnesia about what it takes to build wealth. As a result, some of them end up watching as large portions of their assets evaporate. They have no healthy fear—of going broke, of losing the money machine, of losing their lifestyle and the status that comes with it.

One common factor among many (though not all) of those who don't appreciate their wealth is age. If you have money early in life and then the cash-flow faucet shuts off later on, it can be a brutal shock. It's actually easier the other way around: for someone to grow up in poverty and then have money later in life. In that scenario, individuals usually have much better coping mechanisms for whatever life throws at them.

The bottom line is this: It is a rare accomplishment to accumulate $30 million, $50 million, or $100 million in after-tax wealth. If you've made it, you need to have a conscious awareness of what it takes to reach, then stay at, that level. It isn't nearly as simple as it looks. A clear understanding of wealth—and where it comes from—is a "pearl of great price." It is only upon pain of loss that we realize what it truly takes to amass a fortune.

If you have wealth, then I suggest you become a grateful and good steward of it. If you do those two things, you'll hang on to your position and be in a very small minority.

OXBOW NOTE

Balance isn't always easy to find or choose—especially when it comes to money. Somehow a lot of people have a harder time saying no to risky investments than they do to an extra slice of cake or one too many cocktails—even though the fallout of one terrible investment mistake can last a lifetime. If you are an investor, somewhere along the line you need to get settled with the way you manage your assets, finding a balance that allows you to both achieve gains and be at ease with your strategy. For an in-depth look at concepts and strategies every investor should consider in the continuous quest for financial balance, contact us at OxbowAdvisors.com to request a free copy of my book, *Stay Rich with a Balanced Portfolio: The Price You Pay for Peace of Mind*.

Chapter 6

BEWARE THE EGO

Hand in hand with a lack of appreciation of wealth is the problem of the ego. In fact, of all the factors that lead to significant loss of money, ego is often the common denominator.

It typically starts with a genius complex. Many individuals who've come into great fortunes can't imagine any factors in that outcome beyond their own intellect and drive. Once they're successful in the highly competitive business world, this attitude tends to get worse. Everyone wants to be the latest, greatest, most brilliant investor—first to find, buy, or grow something shiny and new. These people want to be included on every invitee list and social agenda, and they crave respect. This "game" can be intoxicating, even addictive.

We see this a lot in investors who feel as if they have some particular knowledge or insight that's better than everyone else's. It's a mighty big market out there with a lot of smart players, so what makes them so sure they are right? Usually the answer can be boiled down to one word: ego.

The next symptom of an overactive ego is myopic vision. When looking at a prospective or ongoing investment, an astute investor can step back and analyze the situation without bias. The ego-driven investor, on the other hand, can't do it. They refuse to take that step, to consider the big picture, or to look at outside factors. Even when it becomes obvious a situation is untenable, they stay focused on the close goal of personal success and vindication over everything else.

Of course the same people who won't seek perspective on their investments also won't seek or listen to good counsel. They have a unique kind of selective hearing. In my 40 years of watching people squander it all, most of the people who lost a lot shared this quality of being unwilling to hear reason. Each thinks they've discovered some sort of holy grail of investments—a venture that can't miss. They tune out anyone who says differently and chase after bigger and bigger fortunes.

Their listening skills go to zero, often with disastrous results.

A last common example of those ruled by the ego are the

investors who become obsessed with name or personal brand recognition. A case in point is the restaurant business. I've seen countless people throw good money after bad in high-dollar restaurants because they want their name on the door. They lose money month after month, year after year, and yet continue to maintain the facade that their business is successful.

This variety of egomania carries over into needless construction. Have you ever noticed a vacant piece of land where a building goes up, then nobody moves in? Somebody, somewhere decided it would work, ignored all counter-indications about the location, and built a structure anyway.

And don't forget those who buy—and cling to—stocks that keep falling. These owners will often pour large sums of money into businesses that will never make it. Their egos won't let them stop putting money into the deal. They don't have the capacity to go back and admit it didn't work.

I watched a great California investor take most of his money and pour it into a business that was totally unlike the first business he owned. He sank everything he got from the sale, plus his other assets, into the new business. It failed. He became depressed and ill. I've always wondered if the bad deal might have been a contributing factor to his illness.

The most disheartening thing about ego-driven mistakes is the trail of problems and heartache they invariably leave behind. At Oxbow, we've seen spouses go back to work and prime real estate liquidated because money got tight. We've seen families break up and friendships fracture, largely because ego reared its stubborn head. Over the years we have warned numerous investors that they were doing the wrong thing or making a bad investment. But even after the money was lost, ego wouldn't let them admit—or learn from—their mistakes.

What many investors fail to realize—at least until it's too late—is that this doesn't have to happen. Act in moderation. Remain cautious and curious. Be willing to consider the possibility of the occasional misjudgment. Know when to course correct. Seek wise counsel and listen. Value those in your inner circle who ground you. Above all, have a little humility. If you can keep your ego in check, you will be much better off.

It's been nearly 3,000 years since Solomon wrote that "pride goes before destruction and a haughty spirit before a fall," but these words of wisdom continue to ring true today.

Chapter 7

THE BIG DEAL

When people make a lot of cash quickly, many set out immediately in search of another investment—the next big deal. They usually move too fast on it, and it turns out to be a mess. Business owners who sell their companies are especially vulnerable to this because most of them are feeling a little lost after the sale. They're not sure what life after the business is going to look like, they've got a mountain of cash, and the minute news gets out about their newfound wealth, "opportunities" start coming at them from every direction. The potential deals and business opportunities are seemingly endless—and everyone is telling them their particular deal is too good to miss.

All too many people jump at the first or second offer presented to them, no matter that it requires a significant investment. And that major capital investment effectively reverses the liquidity benefit the investor originally had. Just like that, they're converting liquid net worth into an illiquid investment, letting all that money flow away into a potentially risky endeavor.

One example I witnessed played out like this: A business owner was offered a huge premium for his business. His situation at the time was essentially a monopoly, as he was the only franchise in the city where he lived. He decided to sell, and there was plenty of money for living happily ever after. Very soon after the sale, however, he was offered the chance to buy a business in an industry he'd always loved—one in which he might be considered a hobbyist. This business was not a monopoly. Then there was an economic downturn, one that resulted in cash call after cash call (a company asking existing shareholders for additional investment money). The man owned and operated the business, the deal took most of his proceeds from the original sale, and he soon found himself in a financially precarious position.

There's a simple rule of thumb that every newly liquid business owner should adhere to in almost every "big deal" situation: *Never put up more cash than you can afford to lose in the new venture.* Seriously consider the impact that limited liquidity can have on your ability to maintain your lifestyle in a worst-case scenario.

Even when you're dealing with a business you know, the deal should be financed so as not to impair your liquid capital.

It's important to take the time necessary, including the use of outside resources, to evaluate deals as they're presented—and to do so with capital preservation as a priority. We have seen many people lose significant wealth because they didn't carefully and thoughtfully consider each step.

In too many instances, investors could have moved forward with financial security if they'd just declined to bite quickly on a "big deal." They would have benefited from less haste and a more careful appraisal of their options, with an eye toward long-term financial security.

THERE WILL BE ANOTHER

One of the great myths of investing is the idea that there's a finite number of good deals on worthy investments. This is not true. Deals will come and they will go, and there is always another out there for those who have patience and liquidity.

Successful investors are usually slow to pull the trigger. They take their time and review all angles of the deal. They test out their theories with knowledgeable and trusted advisors, always remembering to assess and project what might go wrong. Most of the bad investment decisions we've witnessed over the years have come from moving too quickly and chasing the crowd.

At Oxbow, the first thing we recommend to investors with significant new liquidity is that they sit tight for a period of time. There's nothing that needs to be done so quickly that you must run out and chase it. Instead, ice the money, sit back, think about the future, and think about what you want from life and from your money.

Chapter 8

THE TROUBLE WITH FAMILY MONEY

I've lost count of the number of times I've had a second- or third-generation heir in my office who tells me their family was once extremely wealthy. They remember growing up in or visiting mansions, riding horses at the family ranch, playing in the sand beside the beach house, or trips to Europe on the private jet. Some can still visit arts centers or hospital wings with the family name on them—proof of great fortunes and largess in the past.

When I ask, some of these individuals don't know where the money came from—or they answer in vague terms, saying it was made in "oil," or "manufacturing," or just "good investments."

Even more mysterious is the fact that many members of this group have no idea what happened to that wealth—why it didn't last through generations. The fortunes were enough. If each generation had just spent and invested with some good sense, they'd still be intact.

But they're not. The money's gone. In fact, in their 2023 book *The Missing Billionaires*, authors Victor Haghani and James White investigated this phenomenon and came to the stunning conclusion that if the wealthiest Americans from the turn of the 20th century and their heirs through the 2020s had simply spent and invested with reasonable prudence, there'd be close to 16,000 old-money billionaires alive today.

What actually played out is that you'd be hard-pressed to find a single one.

THE PATH OF BROKEN LEGACIES

Complications with regard to large sums of money tend to arise when future generations don't realize the time and effort it takes to create wealth. Permit me this disclaimer: The statements that follow are general and not applicable to all cases—but I've found they are true in far too many. So let's look at how the money and its legacy flow through a family:

The *first generation* of wealth often begins on a shoestring. These individuals typically start a business with little capital and build it over time. They work six or seven days a week, 12–15 hours a day, barely meeting payroll and seeing some tough times. They may nearly go broke, but they get through. In many cases, they carry a lot of debt, and they run scared until they finally find success. For years or decades, they live in small houses, drive small cars, and eke out their living by getting up early, going to bed late, and pushing forward.

Eventually, with a little luck, a lot of hard work, and a burning desire to succeed, these Gen One individuals and couples accumulate wealth.

Enter the *second generation*. Here paths diverge, as some second-generation members take the ball and run with it, further building the company or finding their own paths to success, while others simply aren't capable of rising to the task and put the business and the fortune in a state of decline.

Even though Gen Two children didn't amass the original wealth, most did have a front-row seat to someone who did. By watching their parents, they gained at least some appreciation for what it is to pay the price for building a business. They got to see their parents get up every day, worry, and work long hours. They may also have worked in the business at some point. In fact, there's no way to overestimate the importance of the work they did, in or out of the business. A work history is one of the most reliable predictors of future financial responsibility and success.

Gen Two has the advantage of being present while the

first-generation rainmakers reflect on their secrets to success. The benefits of having direct contact with the wealth creators are significant. In their investments, second-generation individuals may also have the benefit of excellent advice from their parents and their parents' proven advisors.

Third-generation individuals often come into an entirely different world from that of their parents or grandparents. In that world, wealth is a given. They have a total unfamiliarity with how life is without money or means. It's not their fault; they don't know anything else. They haven't had the opportunity to see the tremendous amount of work and toil that goes into accumulating wealth.

For many of this generation, having their every material and financial need met without effort or earning makes it extremely difficult to appreciate money as a commodity that can be scarce. Here again, work plays a critical and predictive role.

Not surprisingly, when the time to make investment decisions rolls around, Gen Three is at a disadvantage. Over and over I see the pattern of later generations making bad investments. For them, everything to do with money is easy come, easy go—they have little to no understanding of risk and consequence, and no depth of knowledge about financial matters. As a result, they have a tendency to make superficial assessments—a precarious position, since they have long been in line to become the decision-makers for family fortunes.

My advice to wealthy third-generation individuals is to find a few mentors who are of first-generation wealth. So often I've seen the third generation lose it all because of a few foolish, albeit well-intentioned, mistakes. Third-generation individuals need to do more homework when it comes to investing. The learning curve is longer than most expect.

PARENTAL RESPONSIBILITY AND THE BRAT FACTOR

If you look into the biographical accounts of most top achievers and rich entrepreneurs, you will find commonalities of childhood work and a strong, even compulsive, work ethic. The most successful investors who continue to make large sums of money are people who are not lazy. They were not spoiled as children, although their wealth may be second generation or even third generation. At an early age they internalized a work ethic, which then served them as they learned how to make it on their own. In my experience, most entrepreneurs and people with wealth work very hard.

That characterization may or may not apply to subsequent generations. The truth is, there's an inherent risk in raising children to lives of privilege that you'll wind up with offspring who lack drive, humility, and gratitude. Nobody likes to talk about this, but I'd be remiss to leave it out. The dynamic involves both children and parents, and over the years I've watched a number of wealthy investors spoil their children from the day they're born until the day they (the parents) die. These children seldom get jobs, are often self-centered, and generally do little but feed from the plates of their parents.

As for the parents of these spoiled brats, their excesses usually start out as expressions of legitimate parental love and generosity. But as the children become more tainted by the lifestyle and a lack of expectation to stand on their own feet, it morphs into something else: gutless accommodation of every childish and young adult whim, no matter how foolish, costly, or destructive.

Parents who are wise about wealth have a duty to help the next generation recognize their privileged status, learn to function with true independence, and adopt purposeful lifestyles. When they do this, many enjoy connected, happy families.

Sadly, those parents are counterbalanced by another contingent—those who are unable or unwilling to convey even the most basic values to their offspring. Some parents aren't even aware of the importance of doing so. Children of this second group often have a hard time seeing the world as it really is—a place where most people don't have the kinds of resources they were born to, and where, sadly, some people will do almost anything to share in their privilege. Rich "kids" of all ages are too often targets for scammers, grifters, and hangers-on. While it's easy (sometimes too easy) to criticize the children of wealthy individuals, it's worth noting that most of their spoiled behavior was set in motion by their parents.

It is a sad thing to witness families in which second- and third-generation brats are clearly just waiting around to inherit. In the meantime, they make horrible employees, horrible spouses, and horrible business people. These children splurge and waste and ransack family fortunes until there is little left.

One of the most poignant stories I've seen demonstrate this tragedy is that of a California client who had a nest egg that could last for lifetimes, plus she'd set up large foundations. But over time, her adult children, through begging and emotional manipulation, got her to lavish large amounts of money on each of them. This dynamic played out over a 15-year period, with the children becoming greedier and more impatient to get their hands on the bulk of their mother's estate. It was tragically apparent that they were just waiting for her to die. The moment she did, they arrived to clean out her fortune. The only bright spot in the entire story is the fact that they couldn't get their hands on the foundation funds. This woman was a great, intelligent, generous human being. She deserved better, but she and her late husband had spoiled their children to such a dramatic extent that the kids became entirely focused on the money instead of on their own accomplishments, their relationships, or the good that might come of the family's resources.

This tale is not a stand-alone, but rather an example that represents many families that have followed a similar path. Instead of fostering legacies of accomplishment, service, kindness, and close family ties, they ended up with bankruptcies, breakdowns, broken marriages, and family feuds. It doesn't have to be this way. In each example I call to mind, there would have been plenty of capital to take care of everyone if the children had just been taught a healthier, more productive way of life.

Yes, I'm being blunt here, but my hope is that someone who reads this will avoid making the same mistakes with their children that we at Oxbow have seen repeatedly over the years.

In closing, I say this to wealthy parents: Teach your children to stand on their own two feet—even when it means saying *no* and holding the line. Nobody wants to be the parent of a 30-, 40-, or 50-year-old brat. Every parent can do better if they keep values and self-sufficiency front and center.

OXBOW NOTE

Because family is such a critical issue to wealth preservation, at Oxbow we excel not just in helping families with money, but in structuring arrangements so that money doesn't disappear in the next generation. For more information about how to approach legacy planning in your family, contact us at OxbowAdvisors.com. For a specific discussion of raising families who aren't tainted by wealth, you can request a free copy of my book *Rich Kids, Broke Kids: The Failure of Traditional Estate Planning*.

Chapter 9

THE TROUBLE WITH
THE FAMILY BUSINESS

Another common wealth-loss tale that plays out in families centers on shared businesses rather than just shared family trees. It starts when wealthy parents, in hopes of keeping the company in the family and strengthening family dynamics, hire their children to work in the business. If the adult child has earned their way through a suitable education, hard work, and a track record of achievement, this can be a rewarding and productive scenario for everyone involved.

It can be, but too often it is not. Too many parents undertake these arrangements in an effort to make adult children who've accomplished little to nothing feel useful and productive. They gift their kids jobs that come with high pay, exceptional benefits, and significant authority. Not surprisingly, some young adults who haven't earned their places confuse these benefits with real autonomy.

Beyond the emotional and psychological pros and cons of having adult children in the family business is the financial toll that these non-contributing children take on the parents' balance sheet. In most cases the parents' inability to refuse lavish support of their children's lifestyles negatively affects their own bottom line. Parents with multiple offspring frequently find themselves spending so much on their children—either as direct compensation for their work or simply to help them out—that their own assets shrink to dangerously low levels.

Worse, even, than hiring unqualified children into the family business are the parents who take things one step further and go find another business for their adult child to run. Whether they buy this other business, invest heavily in it, or leverage personal connections to get in, this is a dangerous game. It may sound like a better plan than financially supporting kids outright, but in reality it often becomes a complicated and expensive endeavor. I've seen such numbers as $10 million, $25 million, and even $50 million decimated when parents invested in businesses "for the kids." For starters, there's usually a huge capital drain, and then, since there is little assurance that the children will be successful, there can be a continual siphoning of assets—all in the name of keeping an heir *feeling* busy and productive.

There's a tremendous amount of money spent trying to make subsequent generations of wealthy families successful. Of course, we all know, deep down, that true success—and the self-esteem that comes with it—can't be bought. It has to be earned. Ironically, it can be very tough on an adult child's self-esteem to know that he or she has to play the career-help game because Dad and Mom are writing the checks. Worst of all, the opportunity to build relationships based on mutual respect is often lost when parents are footing all the bills.

One of the ugliest situations I recall witnessing in my work at Oxbow was a Midwestern family who had a thriving business that was sold for upwards of $50 million. Soon after the sale, each of the four children decided to go into some other business in which they had little to no knowledge. The mother and father decided to lavishly support these efforts, and each of the four children ended up unsuccessful. The tragic result was a tremendous burden of family problems, culminating in the husband and wife divorcing and the children having little to do with Mom, Dad, or with each other. Money can profoundly affect families in unexpected ways, so be very, very careful.

Even if the children are just being "helped" without a salary, it's amazing how much money a family can run through in a year to keep them happy. Seed money for some project or investment, a down payment on a home, a car, loans, lavish trips, and so on can drain assets in a hurry. In some cases I've witnessed parents cut their own lifestyle back in favor of their children, neglecting to protect their own net worth.

One truly great gift parents can foster in their children is a sense of self-sufficiency and self-reliance—and it's done by allowing the kids to find their own way and forge their own path, even when there are failures along the way. In their own business endeavors, these parents often learned more from their failures than their successes—and the adult children need the same kinds of opportunities to develop as independent, resilient individuals. They need to work. They need to experience both successes and failures. As the expression says, "There are only two lasting bequests that parents can give their children: roots and wings."

Do your net worth and your children a favor, and take great care in how you distribute responsibilities in your business and your liquid wealth. Don't end up like so many people I have witnessed: frittering away millions of dollars because they didn't have the courage to show a little tough love and do the right thing for everyone involved.

Chapter 10

FEEDING THE ANIMALS

Once people have acquired wealth, they usually start considering their options for investing. They begin with the obvious: stocks, bonds, and perhaps some alternative investments. In our experience at Oxbow, most investors like to be in control of their destinies, which includes their investments. As a result, they often engage in private deals. Their reasoning is that by investing in private companies they'll maintain a degree of control not possible in public markets. They may recognize the danger of putting all their money into one big deal, so they gradually spend money on several smallish companies. In some cases, they may sign letters of credit on banknotes for certain ventures.

As time passes, this or that company or venture needs more capital. It generally isn't a large outlay of cash, so the investor steps in and takes care of it. Eventually, however, more and more financial needs are fulfilled by the person of wealth, and with every "feeding" of their pet projects, their worth further shifts from liquid to illiquid. By the time the investor realizes there are too many capital requirements in all the ventures that keep visiting the trough of their wealth, the cash crunch is on, and there is little production from the investments.

A number of examples come to mind, but most of them go something like this: An individual with money may have $30 million, $100 million, or more in liquid dollars. They invest in an industry (like retail stores) that they fail to see is in decline. Comforted by the relatively small initial capital investment required, they are confident that success is just around the corner. The entity keeps coming back, needing a little more and a little more investment. After years of declining sales and frequent capital calls, however, they file for bankruptcy.

Most people don't understand that once they start down the path of putting cash into businesses that are losing money, a positive outcome rarely results. The ideas may be great, but it doesn't matter if the operations are bad. These individuals keep thinking that if they can make it one more month or one more year, the turnaround will come. But it rarely arrives, and as they keep feeding these projects, cash keeps getting flushed away.

As in other scenarios we've discussed, there are ways to avoid this peril. Here are four rules that'll keep your cash safe from investments that are always hungering for more:

1. Always maintain greater liquidity than is needed.
2. When evaluating outside ventures, plan out a scenario in which the venture doesn't make it. This view of the worst case will provide perspective on how much to keep in your liquid portfolio.
3. Once the opportunity has been evaluated, set and maintain strict limits on the investment parameters. No seconds; no thirds.
4. Finally, *slow down*. There is almost always ample time to find the right opportunity in private ventures, and careful selection will greatly reduce your strike-out percentage.

Chapter 11

CONCENTRATION IN ONE STOCK

Too many times, people with wealth get caught up (or bogged down) in one stock, either by buying it through a public company or by purchasing large numbers of shares in the open market. If you remember their names, then you remember how high they went, only to come crashing back to Earth again. The main problem is that if, say, one-third of your net worth is tied up in a single stock, then your risk of loss is greatly multiplied.

One of the ways people get too much stock is via the public company route. These individuals either take their private company public or exchange stock in a buy-out. Stock deals usually take place when the publicly traded stock is at or near its all-time high. The acquiring company recognizes (and intends to take advantage of) the discrepancy between the earnings multiple it's paying for the private company and the multiple at which its public stock is trading.

Regardless of how you acquire a lot of one stock, the risk is real—even if it's being sugarcoated by Wall Street or the media (most of whom can see only the here and now). Over the years, many industries have peaked at inopportune times and left the devastation of single-stock owners in their wakes. Here are a few of the more notorious examples and some infamous lines from individuals who were heavily invested:

- Early 1980s, Oil and Gas/Energy: At Oxbow, many said we were crazy to distance ourselves from oil and gas during this time. A quote from a real investor was: "A loaf of bread will go down in price before oil and gas prices go down." But down they came, and many fortunes fell with them.

- Late 1980s and early 1990s, Consumer Staples: This group included soft drink and food companies. "I will keep my Coca-Cola stock, it'll go up 10 percent per year for the rest of my life," is what one owner told me. The reality? The stock spent 15-plus years at basically the same price, and that's without considering the impact inflation had on the value of the position.

CONCENTRATION IN ONE STOCK

- Mid- to late 1990s, Pharmaceuticals: Major consolidations and buyouts resulted in some mistakes holding large amounts of overvalued stocks. Drug company stocks had one of the most spectacular runs ever between 1988 and 1998. Many of these stocks rose seven or eight times in value. Here's a statement from that era: "I could never sell this drug stock because of taxes—and besides, it will go up every year." Fifteen years later, those holdings had lost more than 60 percent of their value. What on earth would keep an investor from rebalancing some of those earnings before the drop?

- Late 1990s to early 2000s, Technology: We saw more investors lose it all during the tech bubble than with any other stocks. A business owner summarized the thinking of the time when he told me, "You don't understand these stocks. They don't have anything to do with current earnings; it's a new paradigm."

- Mid-2000s, Housing: This group was red-hot for about five years, and investors couldn't get enough of housing-related stocks. But, too late for many of them, they finally saw the train coming—the mortgage train. It would take more than a decade for the housing industry to recover.

The unhappy ending to all these stories is that many people were left without security and financial freedom because they allowed themselves to get overcommitted to one stock. They either forgot or never learned the importance of diversification.

The main lesson to be learned here is this: Avoid the risks inherent in concentration in one stock. Recognize the potential downside—even when (maybe *especially* when) it's all hearts and flowers. If you have over 25 percent of your portfolio in one company, you need to take a hard look at that. Rebalance at regular intervals to keep your favorite stocks from becoming extremely costly.

Chapter 12

LISTENING TO WALL STREET HYPE

One would think that some of the best investing advice in the world would come from well-known Wall Street firms. In reality, however, Wall Street is sometimes the source of the worst investment information out there, and the sales tactics of the big New York firms often revolve around making investors feel as though doing business there makes them part of an exclusive club. On the flip side, those same tactics cause people who aren't in on Wall Street action to feel like outsiders in the investment world.

There's a fundamental problem with nearly every wealth-management vehicle Wall Street will offer you, and it's that those tools presume you accept risk to increase your wealth. The truth: If you already have $30 million, $50 million, $100 million, or more, you don't need to take risks. When you do, the dynamic offers all upside for Wall Street, but tremendous potential downside for you. Why would you do that? You can afford to wait, to be choosy, to hang on to some cash.

Your financial advisors' highest priority should not be selling you their latest and greatest investment. It must be ensuring you keep the money you have. Once that threshold is met, your next priority is staying ahead of inflation. After that, well, *then* you can get into more risky business (much more about this in Chapter 13 about base capital).

THE TIME-ALWAYS-WINS PROBLEM

Many Wall Street theories and strategies are based on the premise that as long as you're investing for the "long term," everything will work out. I would suggest, however, that it's imperative to define *which* time period, especially since many firms view long term as 20 years or more. For most investors, this timeframe is neither applicable nor appropriate. When investing, most people don't think in terms of a 20-year plan, because they understand how quickly things can change. There are too many variables involved (and too few reliable metrics) to make an accurate assessment so far into the future.

For the majority of investors, a three- to five-year plan is an appropriate time period on which to focus. Wall Street advisors usually neglect to tell investors that, just like everyone else, they (the Wall Street experts) can't truly know what's going to happen in the future; 20-year time periods can be forgiving, but due to age and other factors, many investors simply don't have this much time.

An example of this timeframe situation occurred in 2000 when a Massachusetts man with tens of millions of dollars decided to invest a large portion of his family's liquid assets in a huge hedge fund recommended by a Wall Street firm. While the fund had a solid performance record, its managers, along with the Massachusetts millionaire, were surprised by the severity of the market meltdown in 2001 and 2002. By the time the man realized how poorly his investment in the fund was doing, it had closed its doors. That investor lost more than 90 percent of his original investment, and his lifestyle (and that of his family) was significantly impacted.

In this vein I'm reminded of a quote attributed to Mark Twain, who was notoriously unsuccessful in his investing and learned to worry more about capital preservation than growth. In his words, "I am more concerned about the return *of* my money than the return *on* my money." (During the Great Depression, U.S.

humorist Will Rogers echoed Twain's quote in a newsreel and is often mistakenly credited with the aphorism.)

THE ONE-SIZE-FITS-ALL MYTH OF ASSET ALLOCATION

One of the favorite selling points on Wall Street involves asset allocation. The theory is that an investor needs a certain percentage of their money in stocks, with a subcategory of large-cap stocks, small-cap stocks, value stocks, growth stocks, income stocks, international stocks, and emerging market stocks in numerous categories and countries. The variations are endless, but the reality is that, regardless of allocation, most stocks usually go up or down together. There are surely some differences, but if the market goes down, then just about every category suffers. All the variations look good when packaged for an investor to review, but most wealthy people need to focus on preserving their hard-earned capital before they focus on growing it.

This emphasis is the reason a large portion of assets should be invested in income (or alternative income) securities and cash—to offset the likely volatility associated with global stock markets.

If you're wondering why Wall Street often overweights stocks, it's largely because brokers make more money that way. Room should always be made in a portfolio mix for cash and short-term-income items.

One of our long-time investors at Oxbow likes to tell us, "I always have part of my money in the shade." It's a simple philosophy that draws remarkably little attention at dinners or cocktail parties. While no bragging rights come with safety, it serves a high purpose. Warren Buffett is a big fan of cash flow—and keeps much of his companies' value in cash. He looks to take advantage of situations where cash is needed and never underestimates the value of liquidity.

Other investment vehicles promoted on Wall Street are the "privates"—i.e., private equity, hedge funds, and private real estate funds. The missing ingredient in these investments, again, is liquidity.

THE PRIVATE EQUITY PITFALL

Another example of the pitfalls associated with Wall Street's "long-term-oriented" investment advice occurred when a wealthy individual in the Midwest had more than $100 million, most of which he was ready to invest. Initially impressed by opportunities with well-known Wall Street companies, he began dropping money into a variety of hedge funds and private equity deals in real estate partnerships.

Later, after sustaining disappointing losses of more than $30 million, he decided to change his strategy and invest his capital with a new firm. However, he was unable to withdraw much of the money sunk into these alternative investments, and he continued to receive capital calls for his illiquid partnerships many years after leaving the Wall Street firm. To make matters worse, the investment house was unable to tell him the true value of the underlying private equity and real estate investments.

A lot of smoke and mirrors were involved in the fleecing of that fortune.

One last "principal" point needs to be made here. If you set your investment horizon to a reasonable timeframe for your situation—and manage to allocate your assets appropriately while preserving liquidity—the next issue to deal with is the percentage of the portfolio that can be distributed without erosion of principal.

Many Wall Street advisors recommend taking out a set percentage each year, regardless of market conditions or performance. The problem with this thinking is that assets go down during market declines, and it's difficult to return to the original principal amount if consistent distributions are taken from a smaller asset base. There is a finite amount of money that produces a predictable flow, and it's prudent to review account distributions periodically to be sure your principal is not being eroded.

In the same way a business owner reviews expenses and determines whether or not they will harm the company's bottom line, wealthy investors must evaluate their expenses with an eye toward preserving capital. Unlike the business, which is a growing entity, this invested sum is difficult to replenish.

As in other scenarios we have discussed, patience, watchfulness, and good guidance can prevent loss of capital. Wall Street is ultimately about sales, and the hype is endless. Guard your wealth, and don't be afraid to be conservative.

OXBOW NOTE

First-generation wealth earners need to constantly guard against schemes designed to separate them from their wealth. These tests of your judgment don't always come in the form of shady characters with questionable reputations. Many show up polished, with the sheen of Wall Street on them. Just remember the caveat about buyer beware. If you'd like a free copy of Oxbow's analysis of the scams designed to separate you from your money, *Wall Street Lies: 5 Myths to Keep Your Cash in Their Game*, contact us at OxbowAdvisors.com.

Chapter 13

THE BASE CAPITAL/INVESTMENT CAPITAL DIVIDE

One of the most misunderstood concepts in the investment arena, applicable in all of this book's chapters about investment options, has to do with distinguishing between base capital and investment capital. For wealthy investors, base capital is that part of the investment funds that should not be put at risk. At Oxbow we call this capital the foundation of your total liquid asset base. Other names to remember it by? The safety net. Your peace-of-mind money. The if-all-else-goes-to-hell fund.

Whatever you call it, it should be non-negotiable.

Base capital is what produces income, takes care of living expenses, pays for insurance, covers medical expenses, and funds the other expenses of day-to-day life. The first stage of any investment plan should be the construction of a base capital portfolio, done with the understanding that this money will not be compromised. This means the answer must be, "No, the base capital is off-limits," when investment deals, adult children, and other financial requests come your way.

Once your base capital is in place and you're confident there's enough money for day-to-day living—plus a buffer in every case—then and only then should you shift your emphasis to investment capital.

THE SECRET TO OPTIMISTIC INVESTMENT

Consider an investor with $30 million who has a lifestyle that can be maintained using $15 million in base capital. It would be patently ridiculous for this investor to risk their lifestyle by having a mere $5 million or $8 million in base capital and some $22 million to $25 million in investment capital. But many investors do just that, in a total disregard of, or through a failure to understand, the difference between the two classifications of money.

Investment capital is that portion of one's assets that can be put at risk. That risk can be relatively small or in some cases it can be quite large, as long as it doesn't affect the base capital assets you have in place. Investment capital is that portion of wealth that can move up or down and have little impact on your daily life in the long or short term. When the parameters are set up correctly between your base and investment funds, investment capital can fluctuate 10 percent, 20 percent, even 30 percent, and not have a significant impact on your overall well-being.

Almost all top-notch investors have a stash of base capital, which they rarely (or never) touch. This cache may not be working very hard, but there's a psychological comfort level that comes from knowing that a portion of your capital isn't going to move around in value. In our opinion at Oxbow, this gives you the ability to deploy your investment funds with a greater sense of optimism. Win or lose, you will be okay.

It is a dangerous mistake to assume all your money belongs in one pot. Even worse than individual investors who don't make a healthy distinction between base capital and investment capital are people in the financial services industry who don't make it. This often happens, especially among financial advisors who don't have a lot of net worth themselves. A high level of net worth should bring a new perspective regarding financial risk and an enhanced appreciation for protecting the base.

COSTLY MISTAKES

A prime example of what we at Oxbow have seen looks something like this: An individual starts out with $30 million in liquid assets. They initially set up in a position where $15 million is base capital and $15 million is investment capital—an excellent start. This structure will likely suffice to cover all basic needs, expenses, etc., while at the same time allowing $15 million for investments. In the course of investing in various business deals, stock markets, real estate, etc., the investor uses up the full allotment of investment capital. That's when the trouble starts. Another deal comes along that sounds too good to miss, and the investor dips into the base capital to get in on it.

We have seen this scenario play out over and over again, with investors returning to base-capital funds so they can continue dabbling in—or desperately chasing—elusive returns in high-risk investments.

Ultimately, base capital dwindles. After a period of five years or so, the individual who had it made is now down to just a few million dollars of base capital—and all the other money is invested (much of it illiquid). This person cannot maintain their lifestyle on that reduced base capital's returns, and so the "$30 million and broke" cycle repeats. These individuals keep waiting for their ship to come in from the investment capital—all the while bleeding base capital, quixotically assuming they will replenish it as soon as one of the deals comes to pass. If the deals don't play out (as happens more often than not), it's just a few years before this investor is scrambling for liquidity.

Look, investing opportunities will always be there. New deals, new businesses, new real estate—they're always presenting themselves to people with money. But if you don't first meet your base capital needs, you'll never be in the right frame of mind to become a wise investor.

Respect your base, and recognize it for what it represents in a life of wealth: peace of mind.

OXBOW NOTE

Strange as it may sound, holding on to wealth often turns out to be harder for families than getting it in the first place. The majority of wealthy Americans fail to keep their fortunes in the family for more than a single generation—and many don't make it that far. If you'd like a free copy of my book *The Psychology of Staying Rich: How to Preserve Wealth and Establish an Enduring Legacy*, contact us at OxbowAdvisors.com.

Chapter 14

THE BIGGEST NEED: UNDERSTANDING RISK

People who take big financial risks have always intrigued me. I wonder what they were thinking. In countless cases, we at Oxbow have seen investors take risks when there was absolutely no reason to do so. Their assets were substantial—enough to last at least a lifetime. In spite of that, they felt the need to show the world (or just themselves) that they could win again—to prove their first fortune wasn't a fluke.

Watching these tragic stories play out, I've come to the conclusion that many people do not truly understand risk. They don't have any concept of how it might feel to wake up one morning and discover that 40 percent (or more) of their net worth is gone—or at least temporarily out the window. They know these losses can happen, but they're so blind, arrogant, or misguided that they can't imagine loss happening to them. Even when they see other people taking major risks and coming up empty-handed, they don't learn. Someone else's disaster is never a cautionary tale—just the story of a poor sap who made a big mistake.

I can tell you from 40 years of watching wealth come and go that it can slip away from even the brightest, boldest, or biggest investor. You simply cannot account for every factor that can come into play when you assume a risk. Disaster can befall anyone who gets overextended and forgets the importance of keeping bulletproof base capital.

When an individual is investing a small sum, or a young person is starting up a new business, there's sometimes a need for above-average risk. But as investors mature and their assets mature with them, the need for excessive risk declines. There's no need to take on an inordinate amount of risk just to reach the next level when you're likely to get there anyway, with minimal exposure and a little patience.

To quote 17th-century French mathematician and philosopher Blaise Pascal, most human misfortune stems from "man's inability to sit still in a room." Sometimes, your wisest move is no move at all.

THE BIGGEST NEED: UNDERSTANDING RISK

SOBERING QUESTIONS

Most wealthy investors are confident they're comfortable taking on some risk. In the long run, though, they have a hard time determining what *some* is. At Oxbow we use numbers instead of words to help sober investors about the reality of risk. For example, if an investor has $25 million, we offer a hypothetical possibility (one that could easily play out at some point in time):

> If we call next month and inform you that your $25 million is now worth $15 million, how would you feel? Would you be angry? Depressed? Would you be filled with regret, wishing you hadn't taken on so much risk? Or would you not care at all?

These are the types of questions that frame the hypothetical of "some" loss into the emotions of real situations.

Another situation where a simple question can shine a light on risk issues is when investors are oblivious to how exposed they've become. I ask most new investors this one first:

> Can you tell me what level of risk is in each investment you have—your stocks, bonds, insurance, hedge funds, commodities, or anything else?

It's shocking how many have no idea. I'm reminded of an investor in the late 1990s who had come into a tremendous amount of money and had never had much to do with the stock market. Within three months he was trading stocks online hand over fist, thinking it was one of the easiest things he'd ever done in his life. We couldn't make much headway with him because, for a while, every day was another success story. But a few years later, when I visited him in California, I learned he'd lost almost 80 percent of his money—and had actually put his lifestyle in jeopardy. Understanding risk was not part of his overall frame of reference. The fact that he also showed signs of having a gambling addiction didn't help matters either.

Many, if not most, investors have no idea the level of risk they're undertaking (yes, in this context I use the word "undertaking" intentionally). Sometimes they don't bother to find out. Sometimes the risks are veiled by the person bringing the investment. Sometimes they take advice from individuals who don't know enough to offer perspective. They may be told that there is X amount of risk when in reality that friend or informal advisor knows nothing.

Amateur investors think they understand risk, but we too often discover that they can't fully understand what they've gotten into until they get burned. Many have been given a quick risk summary by Wall Street people—a summary designed to get them to accept and move on. It may be that they don't start to ask better questions or scrutinize their advisors until they've suffered a loss.

THE BIGGEST NEED: UNDERSTANDING RISK

Another set of questions that can help sober investors are those about more subtle risks. I ask if a new investor knows of an embedded risk that might not be obvious to an outsider. Or if they can explain how one-time or black swan events could affect their investments. Very few investors have considered—let alone worked through—these types of problems. It doesn't help that Wall Street brokers, planners, and advisors offer oral, off-the-cuff summaries of risk rather than true analysis. Many investors are at the mercy of a low-level guide's assessment—and there's a good chance that person isn't even involved in the investment decisions. Wall Street's front-facing players are all about sales and buoying optimism. Somewhere deeper in the machine, there are other individuals guiding the path of the money.

At Oxbow, we do things differently. We actively choose each investment in our own research group and determine what the risk is regarding a particular item. So if, for instance, you own a certain investment that we chose for you, we have parameters in place based on various scenarios about what can happen with it. We give each investment a multiple-scenario review to look at best cases and worst cases alike. Most people on Wall Street are selling somebody else's wine and don't really understand (or care) what they're putting the investor through. As an investor in their system, you need to understand that the deck is somewhat stacked against you—that you may have to work to get answers to the essential question of, *What is my true risk in this investment?*

It's not impossible to navigate these waters, but it takes time and due diligence on your part, and it means asking questions of the person who's supposed to be in charge of your investments. In addition, I would recommend that you not use third- or fourth-party people who become layers between you and the decision-maker who's actually taking risk on your behalf. It's important, as much as possible, to determine what the person who makes the final decisions about your investments is thinking.

Oxbow has an investor in Florida who, on his own, buys a number of small companies with low levels of market capitalization. This has nothing to do with the money we manage for him, but is done through the money he manages on his own. While he does know a lot about the companies, he knows precious little about the many macro factors of investing. At times, investors need to know more than just what's going on with one particular investment. They need to understand where they are in the current economic cycle, the ramifications of where this particular cycle is now, and what to expect in the next 12 months.

We have a saying at Oxbow that goes something like this: "If you lose investors, lose them because you didn't make enough money for them, but don't lose them because you lost their money." Most people don't do well with losses. They think they've got risk in their blood, but they don't. Studies show that people hate losses more than 2.5 times as much as they like gains. It's a matter of basic psychology that the pain of losing money (or anything) is greater than the euphoria of winning. The vast majority of people are like Lucy of *Peanuts* cartoon fame. They don't want ups and downs. They want "ups, ups, and more ups!"

THE RISK ROLLER COASTER

At Oxbow, we usually have a few investors who are quite risk-averse. But as they watch markets get a little firm and go a bit high, they think they're ready to take more chances. We've been through many cycles with this pattern, so we see the same type of behavior happen over and over again. They want to sell everything at the absolute lows in the market, and then they want to buy something at the absolute high. We know that every time we get to the bottom of a market, one of our investors in the Midwest will be calling. His call has become one of our great "buy" signals, because he invariably asks us to sell when it's the best time to be buying (and he asks us to buy when it's time to sell). The ironic part about it is that he never seems to learn—he cannot see his own pattern.

So there's a basic need in each investor's life to determine risk and to align investments so they work with your comfort level rather than against it. As you sort this out, beware letting someone of dubious credentials try to tell you what your risk profile should be. You are the one who has to sleep with it and live with it. Make sure you know the levels at which you can lose real money. Follow the advice of this chapter and ask lots of questions. Your willingness and ability to do so may end up being a saving grace for you and your investment portfolio.

OXBOW NOTE

In my book *Your Money Mentality: How You Feel About Risk, Losses, and Gains* I explain how investing is not linear and that successful investing sometimes goes against conventional wisdom. From my years of experience, I walk investors through the highs and lows of the market to help them determine their own money mentality. If you'd like a complimentary copy of this book, contact us at OxbowAdvisors.com.

Chapter 15

LIFESTYLE CHANGES

If you've sold a business and come into newly liquid wealth, it's time to buckle up. Because along with the money, you're going to experience significant lifestyle changes. Not all of them will feel like the big wins you're expecting, and this is a truly precarious time for your newfound wealth.

As I mentioned in earlier chapters, much about how the new rich spend tends to be tied to how they got the money. First-generation wealth-holders are typically selective about how they spend. They know the toil and effort it took to amass wealth. Second-generation wealth-holders can certainly feel the same way, but those individuals have a tendency to be less frugal than their parents—and may extend misspending to include more homes, bigger homes, and more flamboyant lifestyles. And then you have the third generation, far removed from earning the money and prone to spending it like water. This is the generation that's always surprised when they discover the financial well is running dry.

A TIME TO GO SLOW

Beyond generational differences, there are behavioral ones as well, and many of these happen in those first two years after the money comes in—a period when, despite the wealth, it's easy to feel as if life is in a downturn. This is typically the time when the wealth earner stops working—or at least sees a dramatic shift in schedule. The phone doesn't ring as often, there are no meetings to attend, and there's nobody from the office desperately needing guidance at all hours. The shift from being the center of a business universe to sitting on the sidelines can make even the most grounded business owner feel adrift.

Even more isolating can be the discovery that some relationships change when you become independently wealthy. Some of your old friends may feel jealous or even resentful. Some family members will be quick to ask for gifts or loans. Some colleagues and acquaintances will gravitate closer to you, some will move further away, and either way you'll know it has to do with the money. You may even find yourself suspicious of strangers—sometimes for good reason, as it's not uncommon for unethical people to try to finagle their way into the lives of the newly rich.

In many cases, these social shifts are temporary. You'll get more comfortable with your new schedule. True friends will get past the change in your bank balance. A few well-placed *no* responses will let relatives know you're not going to become an ATM. You'll find ways you can be generous to others that are comfortable and rewarding for you. But it all takes time, and when you're sitting at home, waiting for the phone to ring, checking your bank balance, and feeling very alone, this stretch can feel like a long one.

My advice, as with so many other aspects of newfound wealth, is simple and proven: Sit tight. Make small moves. Get comfortable with the luxury of having free time and financial resources. Try out a new hobby or activity, or just get dressed and go sit in an office, so your spouse—who may be entirely unprepared to have you underfoot all the time—can make adjustments, too. As long as you don't blow anything up with overly bold moves during this transition, you'll find a new normal in which your money and your time feel well invested.

A TIME TO GUARD YOUR BASE

Among the most concerning changes we see at Oxbow after an investor's windfall are those that involve new and extravagant spending, expensive travel and real estate plays, and an almost total disregard for the integrity and preservation of the asset base. It's very easy for a person with considerable wealth to end up with only moderate wealth just by making a few unnecessary and poorly timed expenditures. It happens often. Most of the newly rich don't have enough consideration for liquidity and how so many of the things they purchase are neither liquid nor capable of producing liquidity when they need it.

Somebody with tremendous lifestyle changes, therefore, can show a balance sheet of $40 million-plus in net worth but have liquid assets somewhere under 15 or 20 percent of that amount. This is when circumstances start to get tricky. Yes, these individuals do have net worth, but they have low cash flow. And if your cash flow can't support your lifestyle, your liquid wealth will continue to shrink, sometimes at a precipitous rate.

The most vulnerable to these pitfalls of wealth tend to be those who come to it without a set of solid core values and a healthy sense of who they are without the money. People who are grounded by those two factors are far less likely to turn their lives inside out just because they've gotten rich. When you're secure in who you are, you don't need to dramatically change your lifestyle to prove anything about your newfound wealth. Self-esteem is a complicated subject and one outside my field, but it's impossible to ignore how many of those who aren't confident in their "old" selves are quick to make top-to-bottom lifestyle changes—typically very expensive ones that they're eager to flaunt.

Over the years I've seen dramatic lifestyle changes involving individuals and couples who suddenly decide to take on extreme overhead in order to "seize the day." It's all well and good—until tomorrow.

When your investable assets—whether they be stocks, bonds, real estate, oil and gas, or a private business—become less than half of your total net worth, it's time to take note. Assets that consistently *earn* are the key to long-term wealth. If your lifestyle changes are such that you end up with substantial assets that take money and don't make it, then trouble is brewing.

Over the past 40 years I've witnessed many people with tremendous net worth who, in their quest to achieve an extravagant future lifestyle, manage to blow their current, comfortable lifestyle along the way. This outcome always ends in regret.

Remember this: No matter how much money you have or how many things you have, there will always be someone—probably many of them—who have more. The idea of changing lifestyles in order to achieve prestige, respect, and equal footing with the elusive Joneses (who probably don't think about you at all) is ultimately a frustrating and untenable pursuit. If you were happy before, you'll find your way to being happy with your newfound wealth—without having to buy your way to it. If you weren't happy before, take some time to work on yourself, to consider what matters most to you and how you define success. Move slowly, and all that wealth will be there waiting for you to deploy with moderation and wisdom once you figure it out.

Chapter 16

HARD TO MAKE, HARDER TO KEEP

One wouldn't think that keeping money would be harder than making money, but in reality, it is. You need to look no further than the financial histories of the wealthiest families in American history (or world history, for that matter) to see it in dollars and cents.

Why is this? In many ways, it comes down to three factors: the ongoing nature of making money, the fallacy that anyone who can make a fortune will be naturally adept at keeping it, and the failure to take responsibility for one's investment choices.

FACTOR ONE: THE BUILDING PRINCIPLE

Making money usually occurs within the framework of a business, income-producing real estate, or an oil and gas investment. Each is an ongoing entity, and so as long as you're involved, you continue to grow (or at least replenish) your resources.

Keeping money, on the other hand, involves an entirely different dynamic. In many cases, it involves the former owner of a money-making enterprise suddenly holding on to tremendous—but finite—liquid wealth. The situation is unfamiliar to the player, and in all too many cases, they immediately begin to misjudge the strength of that money, the risk they can tolerate, and what the big picture looks like.

If you're wondering how any businessperson worth their salt can "misjudge" money, it comes back to the difference between fixed assets and ongoing operating endeavors. In operating mode, people tend to get caught up in making money and not thinking much about spending it. However, once individuals have come into a large amount of wealth (especially if they've sold the business), many shift gears and get caught up in the spending side of things. They struggle to relax and enjoy just being or doing or having. This dynamic has always been interesting to me—observing people, many of them brilliant business owners, who make a lot of money and then somehow become incapable of keeping it.

At Oxbow, we see people every year or so who we know are going to end up on this dead-end street. They made their fortunes, but we can see that they're not going to be able to keep them. They're not focused on *investing*. They're focused on buying and spending.

I recall a fellow in the South who was one of the hardest workers I've ever known. I watched him build up two different businesses through extreme effort and many hours. But after he sold both businesses, he spent all the money. I couldn't understand the reasoning behind it. He is now working on his third company. I hope he's lucky enough to find success again—and that he's learned enough that this time, when his company sells, he can hang on to the money and finally have some peace.

You can avoid an outcome like this by approaching the art and science of investment for what it is: an entirely new and unfamiliar venture. It's not an opportunity to show what you can do—it's a chance to see what you can learn. There are two things you cannot go back in this life and regain. The first is time, and the second is capital. Time loss is indelible—you can never replace it. Capital loss is a bit more flexible—but only just. It is a rare case indeed where an investor who has let a fortune slip away is able to start over and grow another.

FACTOR TWO: FALSE CONFIDENCE

In my earlier book *You Sold Your Company*, I wrote about helping individuals manage their net worth after selling a business.

Many successful entrepreneurs think they can easily transmute their knowledge of a current business into knowledge of the investment business. They've got great confidence—probably too much. In my experience, it's that very quality that gives them trouble in their investments. Unquestionably they are smart. Unquestionably they are successful. But their intellect and past success can combine to lead them into financial quicksand.

Let's look at the ways this comes to pass:

- **A Beat-the-Market-or-Bust Mentality.** First and foremost, most entrepreneurs don't understand returns. Someone, somewhere along the line, has taught them about benchmarks, about aspiring to returns that beat the market. So instead of focusing on retaining wealth, maintaining their buying power against inflation, and making a margin (in that order), they're out there swinging for the fences and taking on tremendous and unnecessary risk.

- **A Little Knowledge and a Lot of Feeling.** Many of these individuals have learned just enough investment terminology to be dangerous. Three hundred years ago Alexander Pope said, "A little learning is a dangerous thing." He wasn't referring to investing, but he could have been. The catch is this: Investing is not like running your own business, where you knuckle down and deal with the basics (and the nuances) of capital, equipment, sales, personnel management, etc. You strive to stay level-headed. You are constantly building, making adjustments to keep the business profitable and growing. There is a wide margin of opportunity to learn and improve over time.

Investment, on the other hand, is heavy with emotion—with fear, greed, and worry. Consequences, when they are meted out, are extremely difficult to recover from. And far too many new multi-millionaires don't recognize the distinction, or the pain, until they've been dealt a brutal blow. At that point, a percentage are so far gone they're doomed to fail as investors.

- **Ignoring the Fundamentals.** We at Oxbow can tell countless stories of smart people who've lost millions. These are personal tragedies of giant proportions. Many of their mistakes come down to having little understanding of how to deal with bad markets and good markets. In general, they simply don't understand how to make correct purchases or correct sales. Our best advice is to be much more conservative than you think you should be. Don't presume you have ten years to learn like you did in the business world. In investing, fortunes come and go in a hurry—sometimes even in a matter of days.

- **Taking Bad Advice.** The primary objective of investing is to maintain purchasing power over the entire lifetime of one's money. If you are speaking with advisors who are telling you different, pay close attention to your potential downside. Your aspiring broker, who may have a brand-new MBA and be looking to break six figures for the first time whilst doling out guidance, is in the chase for wealth. *You already have wealth.* You are not playing the same game as that advisor, and you do not share the same goals. Be wary of any investment component—whether it be real estate, stocks, bonds, or private business—where you can't understand the extent of your risk. Anything with market risk involved must be balanced with conservative investments in the public realm. Unfortunately, many among the newly rich lean on advisors who are looking to make a killing on their wealth instead of seeking to preserve it for them.

FACTOR THREE: RIGHT OR DIE

At Oxbow, we notice that people who have blown large sums of money will blame everyone except themselves. There's an undeniable allure in being seen as smart or right. There's that warm, smug feeling you get when you have (or think you have) knowledge about some fantastic investment that everybody's going to wish they got in on. But focusing on being the first, best, most brilliant, and infallible creates a weight of unrealistic expectation. It can set in motion a drive to constantly top your own (or someone else's) biggest move.

In the end you are responsible for your own welfare and your own financial success or failure. You don't have to be brilliant. You don't have to have a sixth sense about where to throw your money. What you have to do is embrace the process of due diligence. Do your homework. Ask questions. Listen to the answers. Move slowly and carefully. Diversify. Take at least as much time to learn about investing (and what you're investing in) as you would any other business venture you pursue.

The story comes to mind of an investor who placed an inordinate amount of money—nearly 90 percent of his net worth—in one company. The business went under, and the investor was devastated by the many millions of dollars he lost. When I discussed the situation with this man and his associates, they continually commented on the fact that, unfortunately, they got involved with a bad business. Nobody was willing to acknowledge the proverbial elephant in the room—the fact that they'd placed *90 percent of their liquid assets into a single venture*. That reckless and uninformed decision is what cost them their fortune. There is never enough justification for putting the majority of your liquid wealth into any one item or company. Companies fail. Stocks drop. Economies shift. Things happen. That man and his partners were the ones who would have to own their life-changing miscalculation.

In almost every case, investing mistakes can be traced back to a moment when the investor could have said, *I don't want to do that*. But they were either sold a bill of goods or were too convinced of an outcome (no matter how uncertain) to be able to stop their momentum before taking a disastrous plunge.

Twenty-some years ago we received a wire for more than $100 million to manage for an investor who'd sold a company. Against our counsel, this investor then took the liberty of pouring money into various risky businesses, stocks, and bonds. Within a year he'd lost vast sums, and we were lucky to be able to round up $4 million of that money for him to recalibrate his life with. It happens over and over again, primarily because entrepreneurs blindly trust that their business acumen will seamlessly extend to investment knowledge.

All this gives us something to think about when understanding that money is hard to make and even harder to keep. Concentrate on the long term—and remember how hard it was to put those assets together in the first place. It pays to be conservative.

Do yourself a favor. Become a good listener and move slowly. Those two simple, logical steps can help you dramatically change your end results.

OXBOW NOTE

If you recently sold your business, you're as vulnerable to wealth loss as you'll ever be in your life. For a free copy of my book *Danger Time: The Two-Year Red Zone After Selling Your Company* and more books and videos on this subject, visit OxbowAdvisors.com.

Chapter 17

MONEY, PURPOSE, FRIENDS—AND MORTALITY

After observing wealthy people for all these decades, I've come to understand some of the reasons that they—usually in the second half of life—do what they do. I've seen some individuals with large sums go broke and rise again to make even more money the second time around. More often, though, I've seen people go broke and stay broke.

Money isn't everything. We all know this. But I'm convinced that it does have an impact on our psychology—especially as we grow older. Though they seldom admit that running out of money is on their minds, this is a concern most people share. I've seen wealthy individuals lose tens of millions, then fall into deep depression. I've seen others lose their fortunes and then, seemingly out of the blue, get sick or have a heart attack or just die. I believe that part of the reason for these sad developments is the stress of loss. It's tough to admit that, after having it all, you've lost the lifestyle.

One of the greatest lessons a parent or mentor can teach a child or protégé is the proper handling of money. All too often we at Oxbow see investors who have lots of cash but little sense of how to handle it. So over time they waste too much, and eventually it's gone. Example after example comes to mind of older people who we could see were going to blow through their money within 18 to 24 months. In a high percentage of those cases, these individuals ultimately became depressed or ill, or something happened to them that ended their life. We don't have any scientific, empirical evidence of a connection, but we've seen it too many times to ignore or consider it strictly coincidence.

One of the major building blocks of longevity is purpose and meaning. At all levels, we see people who give us hope—those who live long, do well financially, and have fun. In almost all cases they also have tremendous senses of purpose. Some help friends, relatives, their communities, and others. Some give back through faith-related ventures and charities that matter to them. In more cases than not, people with purpose live long and enriching lives.

MONEY, PURPOSE, FRIENDS–AND MORTALITY

On the other hand, we observe that people who are selfish (even stingy) with their money, time, and effort rarely live with as much joy—or in fact to such length—as those with purpose. Those who sow kindness and good deeds in their youth and middle age usually reap a harvest of gratitude and happiness in their old age.

How does this relate to the idea of *$30 Million and Broke*? Here's how: Having purpose has a way of making people more successful in investing. While we can't say exactly why this is, we do notice a high rate of success among people who give back. It's almost as if there's a large circle and the more you put into it, the more you get out of it. I don't offer this comment from a soapbox, but as a long-time observer of the investment world. I've concluded that investors who live with purpose and meaning benefit economically, physically, and socially.

The social aspect is key. Longevity and happiness are both enhanced by having friends and family. People who have strong relationships (including with grandchildren and sometimes great-grandchildren) tend to be happier, have more money, and find themselves in a better place than those who do not. In our decades of investment experience, we at Oxbow have seen that friends and family constitute a key common factor among those who are successful investors. They network, discuss, look at other views, and are continually listening to other people, and they live rewarding lives.

In sum, we see three ways that some people cut their lives short: by losing their assets and security, by lacking purpose, and by being socially disconnected.

Alternately, we see three ways others make the most of longer and happier lives: by being good stewards of their money, by having a sense of purpose and meaning, and by nurturing healthy and close relationships.

Your choices matter, not just when it comes to your bank balance. Find your purpose and your people, and you'll likely find some of the grounding you need to make smart financial choices as well.

Chapter 18

IF YOU HAVE IT, DON'T LOSE IT

How much money is enough to last a lifetime? One person's million might be another's $10 million or $100 million. But I am telling you right now that if you have enough wealth for the title of this book to represent you—$30 million or more—it is enough.

Or at least it can be.

Over the years, I've seen one person after another operating on the false assumption that the wealth they have—whether it's $30 million, $80 million, $100 million, or far more—is not enough. Some people, in this as in all things, are incapable of being satisfied. The irony of that greed and drive for more, more, more is that it often leads to profound losses. Over the years, we at Oxbow have had to bear witness as billions of dollars have been wasted in the pursuit of . . . more millions.

One of the craziest situations we ever saw was in the Southwest, where a family sold a company for $200 million and yet ended up with just a few million dollars eight or nine years later. The sad and ironic fact was that we could have set them up for a tremendous amount of incoming cash flow for the rest of their lives. They would have had complete peace of mind—security and even luxury from here to eternity. With that kind of liquidity, it should have been a given.

Instead they started shunting off funds in every direction, wasting, buying in, spending, gifting, and always chasing after more. They kept digging a hole, deeper and wider, and letting the wealth run into it.

I implore you to stop and think about what high net worth and liquidity really afford you. It isn't any specific perk or luxury or investment that means the most. It's your freedom. The benefits of being beholden to no one, of having your every need met, of being able to look out for the people you love, of choosing how you spend your days. That kind of freedom is priceless. If you have it, why would you spend your time trying to beat the system to make more? Why would you risk your own or your family's future? Why would you test your relationships by putting the strain of risk and loss and shame on them?

I'm reminded of a couple in the Midwest who made tens of millions over and over again. The husband would take insane risks. The wife would pull her hair out and suffer sleepless nights over their lack of security. Neither of them was happy. They could have put their money to work in conservative investments and gotten on with whatever else brought fulfillment and happiness to their lives—but instead they went round and round in an endless cycle of worry, fear, greed, and anxiety.

When you think about how much is enough for a lifetime, try shifting perspective from the money to the relationships. How much time with your spouse and friends, your children and grandchildren is enough? Instead of thinking about what you can buy or accumulate, think about what you can do—the family trips you can give, the educations you can support, the romantic moments you can create, the weddings and baptisms and birthday parties you can attend and enjoy. In the end, we're all going to die, and what will matter won't be how big a pile of money we leave behind. If you have enough to last your lifetime, don't complicate things by chasing more. Use that wealth to enhance the ride along life's highway for you and for your family.

I close with these simple truths that we at Oxbow have worked to impress on investors for many long years:

- Wealth is hard to come by.

- Wealth is hard to keep.

- You are one of the fortunate few. If you have it, don't lose it.

CONCLUSION

Wealth can be fleeting and ephemeral. There is no guarantee that if you have $30 million you will keep $30 million. Attaining wealth and keeping it are two of the hardest things known to humanity. At Oxbow Advisors, we work nationwide and have been able to see, firsthand and from all sectors of the United States, how billions of dollars get squandered. The problems range from bad investments to ugly divorces, from greedy children to selfish advisors, from fraudulent practices to prison and even death. Any way you can name to lose a fortune, I can likely tell you about someone who did it.

My goal in writing this book has been to describe—as directly and honestly as possible—many of the pitfalls and challenges of wealth management. What I've learned has largely come from watching others. In all too many cases, these people have shown me (and now you) how not to handle large sums of money.

Ultimately, the preservation of wealth comes down to the values you have and the choices you make. If you've made it to the point of having wealth, accept it as a responsibility and be a good steward of its preservation. I'd love to see you maintain it and enjoy its benefits through a long and happy life.

KEY CHARACTERISTICS OF OXBOW ADVISORS

Discipline: Oxbow's investment advisors are disciplined. We don't get caught up in the latest fads. We stick to what is important to the long-term financial health of our investors.

Asset allocation: The oldest and most common investment tool in asset allocation is the rearview mirror. It is great for the past but all too often ineffective for producing results in the future. At Oxbow we don't get distracted by this type of misdirected focus.

Psychology: The key drivers of investor returns are psychology and investor emotions. Irrational thinking and emotions at the wrong time can greatly damage wealth. At Oxbow we maintain a clear and calm approach, regardless of the circumstances.

What if?: Contingency planning assures Oxbow investors that we can handle investments—even if the primary client becomes disabled or, worse, is deceased. Someone has to care for your investments if the unthinkable happens.

Service: Oxbow investors are in the highest wealth category. They demand and expect exceptional service, and we provide just that. Our entire company is dedicated to making life easier and more enjoyable for our investors in every way.

Peace of mind: This is the cornerstone of financial security and personal happiness. With volatility and investment headlines often at peak negativity, it's nice to know that we do the worry part. Having worked with wealth for more than 40 years, we use discipline and our time-tested strategies to relieve investors' stress. Knowing our skills and conservative nature greatly enhances their peace of mind.

If you would like more information, call 512-386-1088 or visit www.OxbowAdvisors.com

ABOUT THE AUTHOR

J. TED OAKLEY, founder and managing partner of Oxbow Advisors, began his career in the investment industry in 1976. The Oxbow Principles and the firm's proprietary investment strategies are founded on the unique perspective he has gained during his decades-long tenure advising high-net-worth investors. Ted's investment advice provides principled guidance to investors from more than 40 U.S. states. He frequently counsels former business owners on protecting and wisely investing their newly liquid wealth.

Ted is the author of several other books, including:

- *You Sold Your Company: Get Ready for Change*

- *Stay Rich with a Balanced Portfolio: The Price You Pay for Peace of Mind*

- *Your Money Mentality: How You Feel About Risk, Losses, and Gains*

- *The Psychology of Staying Rich: How to Preserve Wealth and Establish an Enduring Financial Legacy*

- *Crazy Time: Surviving the First 12 Months After Selling Your Company*

- *Danger Time: The Two-Year Red Zone After Selling Your Company*

- *Rich Kids, Broke Kids: The Failure of Traditional Estate Planning*

- *Wall Street Lies: 5 Myths to Keep Your Cash in Their Game* (with Pat Swanson and Trey Crain)

- *My Story*